Twitter® FOR DUMMIES®

POCKET EDITION

by Laura Fitton, Michael E. Gruen, and Leslie Poston

WILEY

Wiley Publishing, Inc.

Twitter® For Dummies®, Pocket Edition
Published by
Wiley Publishing, Inc.
111 River Street
Hoboken, NJ 07030-5774
www.wiley.com

Published by Wiley Publishing, Inc., Indianapolis, Indiana
Published simultaneously in Canada

For general information on our other products and services, please contact our Customer Care Department within the U.S. at 877-762-2974, outside the U.S. at 317-572-3993, or fax 317-572-4002.

For technical support, please visit www.wiley.com/techsupport.

Wiley also publishes its books in a variety of electronic formats. Some content that appears in print may not be available in electronic books.

ISBN: 978-0-470-54872-1

Manufactured in the United States of America

10 9 8 7 6 5 4 3 2 1

WILEY

Contents at a Glance

Publisher's Acknowledgments

We're proud of this book; please send us your comments at http://dummies.custhelp.com. For other comments, please contact our Customer Care Department within the U.S. at 877-762-2974, outside the U.S. at 317-572-3993, or fax 317-572-4002.

Some of the people who helped bring this book to market include the following:

Acquisitions, Editorial

Project Editor: Kelly Ewing

Executive Editor: Steve Hayes

Copy Editor: Laura Miller

Editorial Manager: Kevin Kirschner

Composition Services

Senior Project Coordinator: Kristie Rees

Layout and Graphics: Brent Savage, Christin Swinford, Ronald Terry

Proofreaders: Laura L. Bowman, Melissa Cossell

Publishing and Editorial for Technology Dummies

Richard Swadley, Vice President and Executive Group Publisher

Andy Cummings, Vice President and Publisher

Mary Bednarek, Executive Acquisitions Director

Mary C. Corder, Editorial Director

Publishing for Consumer Dummies

Diane Graves Steele, Vice President and Publisher

Composition Services

Debbie Stailey, Director of Composition Services

Introduction

Have you heard? All the world's a-twitter!

Twitter is a tool that you can use to send and receive short, 140-character messages from your friends, from the organizations you care about, from the businesses you frequent, from the publications you read, or from complete strangers who share (or don't share) your interests.

As a user of Twitter, you choose whose updates you want to receive — which people you want to *follow.* In turn, other users can elect to follow *your* updates. You can send messages publicly for the entire Twitter community, semi-publicly to users whom you approve to receive your messages, or privately from one user to another. You can view these messages, called *updates* or *tweets,* either on the Internet or on your cellphone.

Twitter has changed and enhanced the way that people communicate with each other, with brands and companies, and with social movements and initiatives. Twitter has empowered users to raise money for people in need, to coordinate rescue efforts in the wake of a natural disaster, and to alert authorities to emergencies and illegal activities both domestic and abroad.

Skeptical of what you can say in 140 characters? The first paragraph of the Introduction weighs in at 41 characters. This paragraph? 137.

You may also find, over time, that you communicate more effectively and that your writing becomes shorter and more to the point. You can say a lot within very little space; and because it takes only a little time to read and update, you may be surprised about how much value you, your friends, and your family can extract from Twitter.

About This Book

We, the authors (Laura, Michael, and Leslie), aren't employees, representatives, or shareholders in Twitter. The opinions that we give in this book represent what's worked for us and our networks, but not necessarily the Twitter world at large. We've been on Twitter for quite a while, and we have a good sense about how people are using it. But Twitter is a living, breathing, and constantly changing dynamic community. Much of Twitter's value comes from the ecosystem of tools built by others to work together with Twitter. Hundreds of these new tools launch every month. Twitter itself may change its feature set, its privacy features, or general direction overnight, which changes the way that people use it.

In fact, from the time we started writing this book to the time we completed it, about a dozen things have changed on the interface, including one complete layout overhaul. Although the layout and the exact location of everything may change around a bit, the basics of Twitter likely will always be the same. After you understand how the service works, you can pretty easily find any feature that may have moved since the publication of this book. ***Note:*** While things change, keep in touch with `@dummies` or our personal accounts

(`@pistachio`, `@gruen`, and `@geechee_girl`) for the latest on our thoughts about Twitter. You can also keep up with the *Twitter For Dummies* community at `www.TwitterForDummies.org`.

We wrote this book to help more people understand, try out, and benefit from the incredible results and opportunities that can happen on Twitter. There's been so much recent fuss over Twitter that you may think it's just a fad. The truth is Twitter's been changing lives for years now. Twitter can be fun, productive, supportive, and surprisingly powerful.

Conventions Used in This Book

In this book, we stick to a few conventions to help with readability. Whenever you have to enter text, we show it in **bold**, so you can easily see it. `Monofont` text denotes an e-mail address or Web site URL. We capitalize the names of Twitter pages and features — such as Settings. Numbered lists guide you through tasks that you must complete in order, from top to bottom; you can read bulleted lists in any order you like (from top to bottom, bottom to top, or any other way).

Icons Used in This Book

Icons in this book point out important tidbits for you to look at, remember, and absorb. In this section, we go over the icons that we use throughout the book to guide you on your Twitter journey.

TIP: The Tip icon points out helpful information that's likely to improve your Twitter experience.

The Remember icon marks interesting or useful facts that we cover in detail in earlier chapters or something that's so important that you need to remember it while you're using Twitter.

The Privacy icon denotes that you should be careful about the Twitter activities being discussed. You may find yourself with a security or privacy concern.

The Warning icon highlights potential danger. When we use this icon, we're letting you know that you should proceed with caution.

Whenever you see this icon, rest assured that we're letting our inner geeks run wild. Here we point out information that's interesting but not absolutely necessary to your understanding of the topic at hand. If you want all the details you can get, read these paragraphs. If you just want to know the basics, skip it.

Part I

Sharing Your Thoughts, 140 Characters at a Time

In This Part

- Understanding what Twitter's all about
- Seeing how individuals, organizations, and businesses use Twitter
- Discovering what you can do with Twitter
- Looking into third-party Twitter applications

You may have heard of Twitter but have no idea what it actually is. Twitter is basically a powerful *mobile* social network that enables you to keep up with the people, businesses, and organizations you're interested in — whether you know them personally or not. It also lets you share what you're doing with the world — everyone from your family and friends to complete strangers. (You'll have to bear with us to find out why you would want to do that.) Harvard Professor Andrew McAfee (`@amcafee`) describes Twitter this way: "With Twitter, my friends are never far away."

And www.Twitter.com itself says that *The New York Times* calls Twitter "one of the fastest-growing phenomena on the Internet." *Time* magazine says, "Twitter is on its way to becoming the next killer app," and *Newsweek* noted that "Suddenly, it seems as though all the world's a-twitter." What will you think?

Every day, we see dozens of new ideas and ways to use Twitter. In this part, we do our best to introduce the basic ideas and explain how Twitter works and why it's so powerful.

Figuring Out This Twitter Thing

Twitter is a fast-evolving, surprisingly powerful, new way to exchange ideas and information and to stay in touch with people, businesses, and organizations that you care about. It's a social network — a kind of map of who you know and who you're interested in (whether you know them personally or not) — that you can access from your computer or your cellphone.

Twitter has one central feature: It lets users instantly post entries of 140 characters or less, known as *tweets,* through the www.Twitter.com site or your cellphone, or by way of the numerous applications that are available for both.

On the most basic level, Twitter is a mobile social network that combines elements of short messaging services (SMS or *texting*), instant-messaging communication tools, such as AOL Instant Messenger (AIM), and blog publishing software, such as Blogger or WordPress. Like blogging, your tweets are generally published to the world at large where anyone can read them on Twitter.com (unless you choose a private account, so that only those you choose can see your tweets). Unlike blogging, you're limited to just 140 characters. Like instant messaging, you can communicate directly with people (through direct messages), but unlike instant messaging, each message has its own unique resource locator (URL), so each message is actually a Web page. Instant messaging also lacks the social network "following" features of Twitter and basic ideas like "publish-subscribe" and one-to-many broadcasting of messages.

Think you can't say anything meaningful in 140 characters? Think again. Not only are twitterers innovating clever forms of one-liners, haiku, quotes, and humor, but they're including links — in 23 percent of all tweets by one measure — and links carry a lot more information and context. Writing 140-character messages seems trivial. But headlines and very short advertising copy are famously hard to do really well — and known to be powerful.

The idea of Twitter sounds simple — even a little too simple. But when you think that millions of people around the world are posting Twitter messages, following other people's Twitter streams, and responding to one another, you can start to see the significance behind Twitter's appeal. True, Twitter can look like it's full of noise. But once you find interesting people and accounts to follow, your Twitter stream shifts from a cascade of disjointed chatter to one of the most versatile, useful online communication tools yet seen — that is, if you take the time to learn to use that tool correctly.

TIP

Twitter is a great way for you or your company to connect with large numbers of people quickly and personally, just like you were having a conversation. In tech-speak, Twitter is a microblogging or microsharing tool; however, you can more easily think of Twitter as a giant cocktail party with dozens of conversations you can join (or start) at any moment. Or, if you prefer a work metaphor, Twitter is like the office water cooler where any number of informal (or formal) conversations can take place.

If you're familiar with blogs, instant messaging, and Web-based journals, you can start to understand what makes Twitter so unique. The Web offers a lot of information. Twitter can turn those long articles, lengthy conversations, and far-reaching connections into easily digestible facts, thoughts, questions, ideas, concepts, and sound bites. In other words, when you have only 140 characters, you have to be succinct.

How Individuals Use Twitter

Tomorrow I begin the archeological dig that is my desk. I will Twitter each item as I process it.

—Author and comedian John Hodgman via Twitter, December 4, 2008 (`http://twitter.com/hodgman/status/1039327071`)

Looking at Twitter for the first time, you might be compelled to ask, "But *why* are all these people, many of whom seem like just random strangers, talking?" At first glance, Twitter seems flooded with disjointed conversations, interactions, and information. You can find news headlines, political debates, observations on the weather, and requests for advice. The idea of Twitter can be a bit confusing for new *twitterers* (people who use Twitter).

People have many reasons for using Twitter:

- **To connect:** Most people start using Twitter to forge connections and be a part of a community. Others just want to be heard. Twitter lets millions of people around the world hear what you have to say; then it lets you connect with the ones who want to hear from or talk to you about your passions, interests, and ideas.
- **To record:** Some people tweet as a way to take notes on life. They use Twitter at conferences, events, or just walking around, and they may even jog their own memories later about something that happened or what they've discovered. For example, if you're walking down the street and you notice a new restaurant you want to check out when you have more time, you might tweet about that. Now everyone who follows you knows about this interesting-looking place, and you have a way of remembering to go back there yourself.
- **To share:** Some people use Twitter to share what they think, read, and know. They may tweet links to great articles or interesting items, or they may tweet original thoughts, ideas, hints, and tricks. Some tweet notes from speeches or classes, and others share choice bits of their inner monologue. Even when this information can get pretty obscure, with millions of listeners, someone's bound to find it informative or interesting.

- **To stay in touch:** Whole families and groups of long-term friends use Twitter to stay in touch. Twitter can send public or private notes to your friends, and it stores all sent messages, which means that you don't lose your thoughts when you close your browser (or your desktop application). Connecting to someone on Twitter is a great way to preserve an initial contact, such as at an event or conference, in a way that lets you gradually get to know that person better over time.

Twitter is pretty easy to actually use, meaning everyone from your 8-year-old cousin to your 90-year-old great-grandma can figure out how to use Twitter and say hello. Because you can access Twitter by using either a computer or cellphone (or both!), it fits into mobile lifestyles and brings you closer to the everyday thoughts of those you're interested in.

How Organizations Use Twitter

Barack Obama's successful presidential campaign in 2008 was perhaps the best example of an organization using Twitter to solicit donations, raise awareness, and call people to action. During the campaign, tens of thousands of Twitter users followed Barack Obama at `http://twitter.com/barackobama`, where campaign staff used the service to provide the then-candidate's whereabouts on the trail and kick off new donation initiatives. (Even though election laws mean the account can no longer be updated, it has hundreds of thousands of followers at the time of this writing.)

The power of Twitter works for much smaller organizations, too. Groups such as churches and local charities can use Twitter to provide an additional way for members to connect, plan, and reach out beyond their immediate community. Preachers tweet about their planned sermons, youth group directors tweet about events, and local soup kitchens tweet when they need help. Whether it's extra hands for a project, far-reaching assistance with a fundraiser, or some other big idea, Twitter can enable organizations operating on a budget to think on their feet.

New organizations have also sprung up through Twitter. Some people have started their own donation campaigns on Twitter and encouraged other Twitter users to donate and then tweet about it. But Twitter isn't just for charities. Enthusiasts of just about any interest have banded together on Twitter. For example, you can find organizations for food and wine lovers sharing recipes and swapping restaurant reviews on Twitter. (You can search for the subjects that interest you on `http://search.Twitter.com`.)

For example, musicians use Twitter to spread the word about concerts, song releases, charitable efforts, and their daily lives as celebrities. (Even Britney Spears has an official Twitter account: `@BritneySpears`.) John Mayer (`@JohnCMayer`) live-tweeted from the Grammies. Musicians working hard to make a name have used Twitter to engage thriving, and involved, fan bases.

Twitter has also been a big help for community efforts. Whether it's Amber Alerts, fundraisers, searching for kidney donors, or rescuing James Buck from an Egyptian jail (`http://twitter.com/jamesbuck/statuses/786571964`), Twitter has shone as a tool for social good. Plenty of people in the world want to lend a helping hand, and Twitter's platform makes it easy, in real time, with a global network of connections.

Businesses That Use Twitter

If individuals, community groups, and nonprofit groups can use Twitter (as we discuss in the preceding sections), businesses large and small can use it, too.

Discount airline JetBlue uses Twitter to advertise fare specials, put out weather alerts, and conduct customer service (`http://twitter.com/JetBlue`). Coffee retailer Starbucks uses Twitter to connect with customers and spread company culture (`http://twitter.com/Starbucks`), as does online shoe retailer Zappos.com (`http://twitter.com/zappos`). Early on, computer manufacturer Dell started a Twitter account (`http://twitter.com/DellOutlet`) to promote special deals on returned equipment and has said that, as of December 2008, its Twitter account has generated over a million dollars in revenue. You can bet, Dell now has many more accounts: `www.dell.com/twitter`.

So why would a business want to establish a presence on Twitter?

- To network with customers and see what they're saying.
- To answer questions.
- To finely tool a company image.
- To poll and pull in feedback.
- To take advantage of an innovative form of 140-character advertising. If you have a limited quantity of something to sell in a short amount of time, you can't find a better channel than Twitter to make it known.
- To take advantage of off-platform benefits. Even a business with **no** customers on Twitter can do this.

But none of these reasons really scratch the surface of why so many people use Twitter. Whether you want to use it for mostly personal or mostly business reasons, or even a blend of the two, you'll find that your reasons for tweeting multiply over time while Twitter becomes more and more useful to you.

TIP: If you're not sure where to begin, you'll be glad to know that many professions are comparing notes about the best ways to use Twitter. For example, ExecTweets (`www.exectweets.com`) shines the spotlight on executives who use Twitter. You can find dozens of industry-specific blog posts and guides on how to use Twitter most effectively. Laura's company started one list of these guides here: `http://pistachioconsulting.com/featured-articles/industry-guides`.

Getting Your Tweet Wet

Having breakfast and getting ready to ride. 6 hours today...

—Cyclist Lance Armstrong via Twitter, December 20, 2008 (`http://twitter.com/lancearmstrong/status/1069006436`)

When you log in to Twitter, a question appears in large print across the top of the screen: "What are you doing?" The most basic activity on Twitter is to answer that question, whenever and however you feel like it. The beauty of this simple question is that you can answer it in so many different ways, and your answer can spark so many conversations.

While you get more comfortable using Twitter, you may find that you ignore the question of "What are you doing?" altogether. That's okay. Twitter is inherently flexible and open-ended, so you don't need to stick to a rigid set of rules. In effect, Twitter is what you make it.

The "What are you doing?" prompt can get some new Twitter users stuck in a rut. Sometimes, twitterers freeze up out of self-consciousness, concern that they're not doing it right, or just plain old 140-character writer's block. You know these Twitter accounts when you see them: The twitterers end up twittering only about what they had for breakfast, that they're leaving the office to go home and watch *Heroes,* or various other mundane life updates that don't spark much conversation. Many of these Twitter users don't end up getting involved in the Twitter culture, and some then stop using Twitter altogether.

If you're brand-new to Twitter and you're ready to try it out, turn to Part II for information on how to sign up, customize your profile, and adjust your settings.

You can get much more value from Twitter — and have a lot more fun — if you just let yourself relax and talk about what's on your mind. Passionate about aardvarks? Send out a few tweets with aardvark facts and see who talks back to you. Have a burning desire to change careers from accounting to roadie for a rock band? Talk about it! You can probably get a response or two.

Tweeting Like a Pro

We'd like to thank you in 140 characters or less. And we just did!

— Twitter co-founder Jack Dorsey, accepting Twitter's Web Award honor at the South by Southwest Interactive Festival in March 2007

Simply put, a *tweet* is what you call the 140-character message that you send out onto the Web by using Twitter.

Why call it a tweet? It's convenient, tying into the whole theme of birds chirping. Also, like much of the Twitter vocabulary, *tweet* is a term coined by the users, rather than the company — evidence of the playful loyalty that avid users have with the Twitter brand.

Twitter limits the length of tweets to 140 characters (letters, numbers, symbols, and spaces), a length that may seem short at first. And it is. How in the heck are you supposed to say anything in this tiny bit of space? How can you distill your company pitch into 140 characters, or review a book or movie by using so few words? With time, you get used to this length restriction. Perhaps one of the coolest things about Twitter is that the more you use it, the easier it is to write short, sharp, clear tweets. As you get more accustomed to tweeting, you find that squeezing thoughts into 140 characters often makes you refine the point in ways you wouldn't have thought of before.

TIP: Some Twitter users have reported becoming better salespeople offline, or better writers, because Twitter's mandated brevity forces you to focus your thoughts into concise, direct sound bites. Because Twitter's communication format encourages brief but engaging ideas, Twitter sparks conversations faster than almost any other Internet conversation format.

Branching Out with Third-Party Applications

At the risk of sounding like a Twitter cheerleader, don't ask "What *can* you do with Twitter?" Instead, ask yourself, "What *can't* you do with Twitter?" From its inception, Twitter has had a very open *application programming interface* (API), which is the geek-speak term for code that lets external developers and programmers weave the Twitter service and functions into other applications and services on the Web. The open nature of the Twitter API has led some people to come up with very interesting uses for Twitter.

The most popular Twitter applications are downloadable client programs that let you manage and update your Twitter feed from your desktop; vying for most popular are TweetDeck (`www.tweetdeck.com`) and Twhirl (`www.twhirl.org`), but people access Twitter dozens of ways, including (about half of average use) Twitter.com.

More than a thousand applications already exist. Some are silly (such as HereBeforeOprah [`http://herebeforeoprah.com`]), some are annoying (such as Magpie [http://be-a-magpie.com]), and some are incredibly useful (such as TwitPic [http://twitpic.com] and HootSuite [http://www.hootsuite.com]). The beauty of Twitter means that even the silly ideas have a chance to succeed, if the Twitter community responds to them. Because Twitter can do so much, so simply, the array of third-party applications offers a nice balance of work and play.

If you want to stick with using Twitter just as a status update service, that's fine. In fact, many people do. But if you want to really maximize your use of Twitter, you may want to check out all the neat ways you can use it — for example, to track expenses, request restaurant reviews, follow gas prices, read the news, find out the weather in your area, give hurricane relief to people in need, fundraise, drive cancer awareness, and a whole lot more. This diversity of use makes Twitter a vibrant community that you can tap into both for fun and for business.

Part II

Hello, Twitter World!

In This Part

- Getting your Twitter party started
- Coming up with a good Twitter name
- Standing out with a unique Twitter profile

Twitter is a deceptively simple yet powerful conversation tool that enables users to broadcast short messages to the world and to connect more closely with people they care about. Intrigued about why this "stupid"-looking tool is so well loved and popular? Then this part is the place to get your feet wet. It usually takes a while of using Twitter to get what about it could be really interesting and valuable to your life. Luckily, Twitter is not only easy to use, but it's also quick to set up and a piece of cake to get going.

In this part, we go over the very basics of Twitter: getting a username, beautifying your profile, and getting yourself situated and ready to start tweeting like a pro in no time.

Signing Up

For many Web services, signing up is the easiest part of an otherwise complicated process. With Twitter, using the site is just as easy as signing up.

To sign up for a Twitter account, follow these steps:

1. **Use your Web browser to navigate to the Twitter Web site at** `www.twitter.com`**.**

   The Twitter splash page appears, as shown in Figure 2-1.

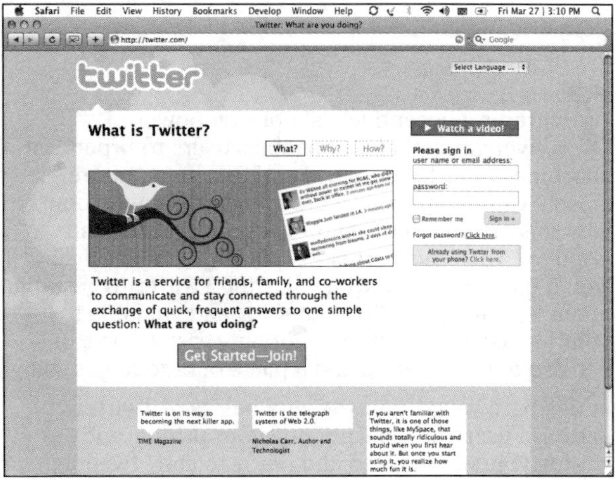

Figure 2-1: The Twitter splash page.

2. **Click the large, green Get Started — Join! button.**

   The signup page appears, as shown in Figure 2-2.

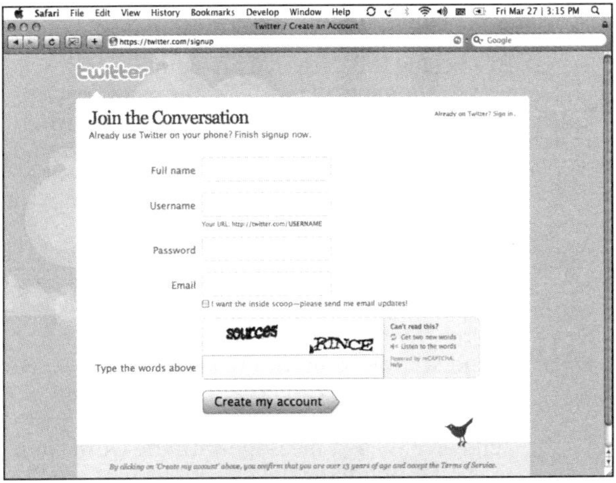

Figure 2-2: The very short and simple Twitter signup page.

3. **Enter your desired username and basic information in the appropriate text boxes.**

   The only information Twitter requires from you is a username, a password of your choice, and a unique e-mail address where Twitter can contact you for notifications. (You'll probably take longer to decide on a username than to actually sign up. We cover how to choose a good Twitter name in the following section.)

4. **Type the CAPTCHA code in the Type the Words Above text box.**

   This step is a standard Web tactic to prove that you're a human and not a spam program.

5. **Click the Create My Account button.**

   By clicking the Create My Account button, you're agreeing to Twitter's Terms of Service. You see a link at the bottom of the page where you can read those Terms of Service if you like, or you can go to `http://twitter.com/tos` to read them.

   You're taken to your newly created Twitter account (see Figure 2-3).

Did you know you can register for Twitter entirely by text from any cellphone? Get a friend started while you're away from a computer — you can create a new Twitter account from any cellphone at any time. Just send an SMS text message with the word "join" to 40404 and follow the directions that are texted back to you to choose a username. Later, go to Twitter.com and look for the button labeled Already Using Twitter from Your Phone? Click Here.

If you already have a Twitter account, **do not** text "join" to 40404 or you will lock your phone into a separate new account. You will not be able to add your phone to your original account until you delete the new one.

Figure 2-3: A Twitter blank slate.

Picking a Name

On Twitter, your username is your identity. Laura's Twitter name, or *handle,* is `@Pistachio`, and it has become the way that many people know her. She's met thousands of people in real life after initially connecting with them through Twitter, and it's not unusual for her to hear, "Hey, Pistachio!" from across the street or across the room at a party. `@Pistachio` has, in effect, become her nickname. If you want a quick glimpse at the search engine "optimization" (SEO) value of Twitter, just run a Google search for the word *pistachio* and you'll find that her Twitter account is one of the very first search results. Crazy.

When we refer to Twitter usernames in this book, we follow the convention of putting an at sign (@) before the name, because that's how you refer to other users on Twitter. (For example, if you want to say that you're reading Laura's book, you might say, "Reading `@Pistachio`'s book." That way, people who follow you on Twitter can easily click over to Laura's Twitter profile, in case they want to follow her, too!) But when you're actually choosing a username, the @ isn't part of it. The only characters you can use are uppercase and lowercase letters, and the underscore character (_).

That story emphasizes that you should think about how you want to be perceived both on and off Twitter and how your username fits into that perception. Twitter is a far-reaching service, and if you get really involved in the culture of Twitter, like the rest of the social Web, it undoubtedly spills over into real life. The days of choosing anonymous handles such as sexybabe44, like you may have when you used instant-message programs or chat rooms in years past, are long gone.

If you can sign up for Twitter by using your name or a variation of it as your username (assuming somebody else isn't already using it), we recommend doing so. It makes your experience with Twitter much easier when the line between online and offline blurs.

For example, if your name is John Ira, you may want to pick a Twitter username such as `@johnira` or `@john`. If users have already claimed those monikers, try adding an adjective or descriptor, such as `@handsomejohn` or `@johntheterrible`. If you prefer for people not to know who you are, you can choose a name that's a bit more generic. You can also use a handle that you've established on other Web sites. You may also want your username to match your e-mail address — for example, if your e-mail address is `doglover1980@whatever.com`, you may decide to use `@doglover1980` as your Twitter name.

Be forewarned! If you choose to use your last name only, like Michael (`@gruen`), you may find yourself without a first name in the eyes of other twitterers.

Using Twitter for your business? You can use your company or business name as your username, and you can fill in that business name in the Name text box on the Settings page for your account. But if you do, be sure to include the names of anyone who handles the company Twitter account in the 160 character "Bio" text box on the Settings page for your Twitter profile. (We cover how to customize your profile in the "Customizing Your Profile" section, later in this part.)

Lean toward using a short Twitter username. ***Remember:*** Tweets are only 140 characters, so when people are replying to you, if you have a longer name, you leave them less room for message content. Twitter limits your username to just 15 characters for this very reason. (For more on how to reply to another person on Twitter, turn to Part III.)

Your Twitter name has power and influence on *search engine optimization* (SEO), or how close to the top of a search results list you appear in a search engine such as Yahoo! or Google. Businesses should consider using valuable keywords as their Twitter names.

Say Hello! Your First Tweets

The entire premise of Twitter is to answer the question "What are you doing?" in 140 characters or less. So, go ahead! Tell Twitter what you're doing right now. Type a message in the What Are You Doing? text box, keeping under the 140-character limit. When you're done, click Update. Congratulations! You've just made your first tweet.

If you're thinking, "Wait, that's it?" you're right: That's it. Tweeting is that simple, but that simplicity makes it powerful. Your first tweet was probably something mundane, such as, "Trying out this Twitter thing" or "Hello there, Twitter. I'm reading *Twitter For Dummies!*"

But while you start to add more and more updates, people begin to see what's going on in your life and what you're thinking about. Twitterers following you or searching for keywords in Twitter, in all likelihood, start talking to you about what you're doing. The conversation starts with those simple exchanges: Talk about your favorite band's new album, your mechanic and how she fixed your car's catalytic converter, or really anything at all. If you've already found your contacts on Twitter, they probably respond to you pretty quickly. If you don't have any followers yet, don't worry; they'll come.

Your tweets, right now, are publicly visible and searchable, even if you delete them immediately after hitting Update. This situation isn't life or death, but be careful. If your updates are unprotected, what you tweet ends up in Twitter Search and on Google, even if you delete it quickly.

Customizing Your Profile

Your public page on Twitter, also known as your profile, is how other Twitter users get their first impression of you, and it can make a big difference in whether they decide to follow you. Take a few minutes to dress it up a little! Making sure that it reflects you or your business makes all the difference when it comes to whether people stick around to see what you have to say.

After you sign up for Twitter, one of the first things you should do is personalize your profile. Make sure that you have

- An *avatar* (a picture that shows up to the left of your tweets, representing you or your company)
- A background image or background color for your home page
- A bio that's 160 characters or less
- A link to anything else you want to share

Some of the best profile pages on Twitter are the ones that give you a look into that user's personality. Someone who loves to ski might upload an image of his favorite mountain range as the profile background and pair it with an avatar that depicts him in ski goggles.

You don't have to bare your soul, but people on Twitter want to know something about you, and the public page is where they can first discover it.

After you log in to Twitter, you can customize your profile at any time by clicking Settings in the top-right navigation bar.

Changing your avatar

Your avatar is displayed to the left of all your tweets, so it's your official face on Twitter. Some Twitter users change their avatars almost daily to different photos of themselves, some users leave their avatars the same all the time, and still others change their avatars according to a specific occasion — holiday-themed photos for Christmas or Halloween, for example. Your avatar is your face, some other picture, or the default oogily eyes emoticon: o_O. It's your choice.

People don't like following back if your avatar is just the default. Show your smiling face and set others at ease!

To change your avatar, follow these steps:

1. **Sign in to Twitter and click Settings in the top-right menu bar.**

   The Settings page opens.

2. **Click the Picture tab (see Figure 2-4).**
3. **Click the Choose File button (see Figure 2-4) and navigate to the picture that you want to upload.**

   Currently, Twitter supports the `JPG`, `GIF`, and `PNG` file formats.

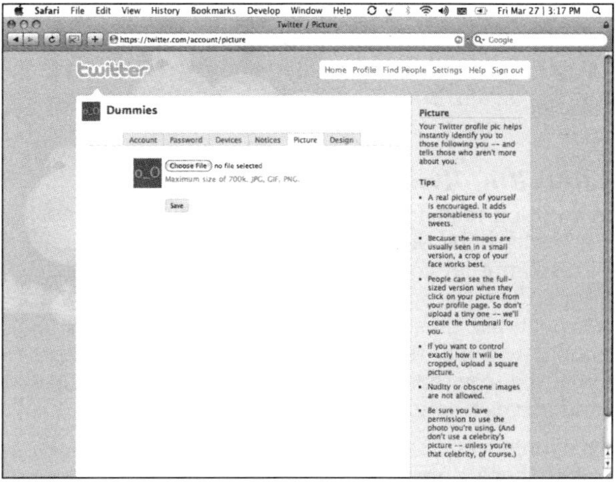

Figure 2-4: Smile for your Twitter avatar photo instead of using the default oogily eyes.

4. **Click the Save button.**

   Your picture is uploaded to Twitter.

The size of your profile image is restricted to 700 kilobytes (which is a rather large image), and Twitter crops it automatically into a square for your public profile. Choose an image that's square or close to square, or make sure that the part of the image you want featured in your avatar's thumbnail version is in the center of the image.

Try to find a picture that's at least 73 x 73 pixels. Otherwise, Twitter stretches the picture out, causing some distortion.

If you upload a photo and it doesn't look quite right, don't panic! Just find a new picture (or adjust the original file) and try uploading it again. You can upload a new picture at any time.

Changing your background

In addition to changing your avatar, you can change the background of your profile page from the default blue to another color. You can even upload an image of your choice (or do both!). You can *tile* an image (make it repeat, like tiles on a floor), make an image large enough to cover the entire background, or choose a smaller image that doesn't cover the entire background (and leaves a solid color behind it).

To change your background by using Twitter's tools, follow these steps:

1. **Sign in to Twitter and click Settings in the top-right menu bar.**

   The Settings page opens.

2. **Select the Design tab.**
3. **Select a pre-made background or use your own image or pattern.**

   The pre-made Twitter backgrounds appear in square thumbnail images inside the Design tab.

   If you don't want a standard Twitter look, but instead want to use a background image or pattern from your computer, click the Change

Background Image link below the pattern images. Then, upload a file by clicking the Browse button and finding your image on your computer.

4. **(Optional) If you want your image to tile, click the Tile Background option.**
5. **If you only want to change your image, click Save.**
6. **(Optional) To customize your text and links, click the Change Design Colors link.**

   You may want to make your Twitter page match the color scheme of your blog or Web site. If you can access the hexadecimal codes on your blog's color scheme, you can enter those same hexadecimal codes in the appropriate boxes. After you finish, click Save Changes to update your colors. If you mess up before you save your changes, you can always hit Cancel or navigate away to retain your current color settings.
7. **Click each of the color swatch squares that you want to change.**

   A note above each square tells you what part of the text or design is affected.
8. **When you're happy with your color scheme, click Save.**

TIP: If you're using Twitter for business purposes, use your background to reflect your company's identity — tiling your logo as the background, for example. Figure 2-5 shows an example of JetBlue's Twitter background.

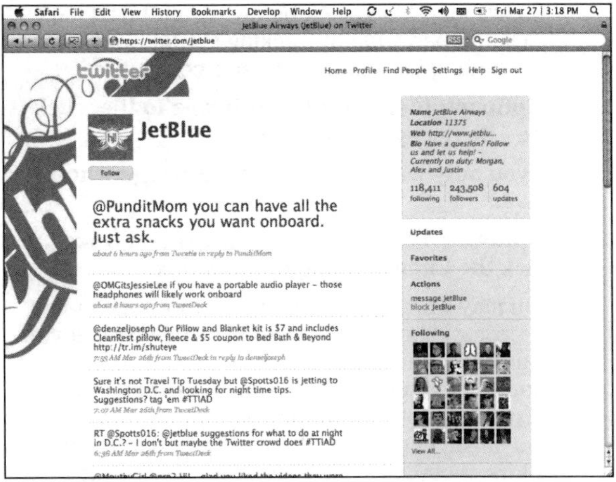

Figure 2-5: A customized corporate background.

If the default themes or images don't appeal to you, or if you're looking for something simpler or more casual, you can find free background images at sites such as TwitterPatterns (`www.twitterpatterns.com`). TwitterPatterns offers a variety of pattern graphics to choose from, all of which are sized specifically to fit Twitter profiles. If you're feeling adventurous, you can hunt online for interesting background images on your own and upload them yourself. Just make sure that they're the right shape and size.

Your background image is almost always overlaid with your Twitter stream, so people usually won't be able to see the middle of the image. Their screen width dictates how much of your background they'll actually see.

Using your background image to expand your profile

Because Twitter's user profiles are so limited, some avid Twitter users take advantage of the background image to add more information or personal links than Twitter allows for in its short Bio section. In many cases, a Twitter user includes a short professional biography, accompanied by more links and ways to connect with that user (see Figure 2-6). This idea is a great way to let people know where else they can find you.

To customize your background image, you need to use a custom template application or create your own template from scratch by using a program such as Photoshop or a free image editor such as Gimp or Seashore. You can also use Microsoft's PowerPoint.

If customizing your own background image from scratch isn't your speed, don't worry! Several sites generate free Twitter templates that are designed just for Twitter neophytes in your situation. One of these sites is TwitBacks (`www.twitbacks.com`), which offers you a fill-in-the-blanks form to create your own Twitter background. Alternatively, you can grab a template from BoinBlog (`http://boinblog.com/2008/07/02/twitter-profile-customization-photoshop-template`). You need Photoshop on your computer to open the file, but it's a fast and easy way to create a template for yourself or your company if you're pressed for time.

Figure 2-6: @Pistachio's extended profile information contained in a background image.

Part III

Tweeting It Up

In This Part

- Following people
- Scouring Twitter for interesting people to follow
- Replying to messages, privately and publicly
- Minding your Twitter manners

One of the neatest things about the Twitter experience is that your conversations, your followers, and your ability to interact with them extend far past the Twitter.com interface into other platforms and even into the real world due to the Twitter community's tendency to plan both formal and spontaneous events. But equally important to accessing your Twitter account from virtually anywhere is understanding how to interact within the community.

In this part, we go over the nuts and bolts involved in discovering, managing, and interacting with the people you follow on Twitter and the people who follow you. Additionally, we give you some hints about how to play well with others within the twitterverse so that you can start having conversations right away!

Finding People to Follow on Twitter

A key part of getting the most out of Twitter is knowing where and how to find people whose Twitter streams are of interest to you.

You can pretty easily find people to follow on Twitter: You naturally browse to people's profiles when you think that something they say is interesting or relevant to you. But, when you start accumulating updates from the people you follow, you'll quickly realize that you need to figure out who's worth following. That process can become complicated because of the large size and diversity of the Twitter ecosystem.

Avid users have countless theories and strategies about the best ways and reasons to follow others. That's the beauty of Twitter: You can make it up as you go along and create your own criteria for building up a Twitter stream.

Twitter is a very personalized experience. No two people use Twitter in exactly the same way, and no two people follow a given account on Twitter for exactly the same reasons. Quite literally, no two people experience the same Twitter because everyone is consuming different streams and publishing to and interacting with different sets of readers.

Twitter is not a single village, as the term *Twitterville* implies. When Laura wrote "Twitter is my Village," (`http://pistachioconsulting.com/it-takes-a-village-to-understand-twitter`), she meant that each twitterer's personal community on Twitter functions like a village. Even if Twitter goes heavily mainstream, you'll still be able to shape your experience there by selecting who you listen to and interact with.

While you become better at your entire Twitter experience, you're continually developing and changing your own guidelines for building your following and follower bases. Luckily, Twitter is built to allow for these changes, so you don't have to miss a beat.

Whether you're looking for business associates, news sources, friendly conversation, or anything else, Twitter can help you surround yourself with people and companies that can enrich your stream.

Look who's talking

When you want to start looking for people to follow, see whether anyone's already talked back to you. If you've already posted some tweets, people may have replied to you. (If you haven't yet tweeted, what are you waiting for? Dive in and start tweeting!)

When someone wants to address you directly on Twitter, that user does so by replying to you. They simply put the @ symbol before your Twitter handle at the beginning of a tweet — that's all it takes to reply. If you're following that person, the tweet shows up in your Twitter stream. If you're not following that person, you can still see any tweets that mention you on the Mentions tab in the sidebar (it's the tab with @ followed by your username on it).

REMEMBER: If you're completely new to Twitter and you've only posted a handful of tweets, you probably won't have any mentions yet. That's okay! You have plenty of other options for finding people to follow (see the next sections).

Searching for people

You can best search for people on Twitter by using one of two methods: Twitter Search (`http://search.twitter.com`) or the People Search function (`http://twitter.com/search/users`). You can also reach Twitter's People Search page (as shown in Figure 3-1) by clicking Find People in the upper-right corner of your Twitter screen's toolbar.

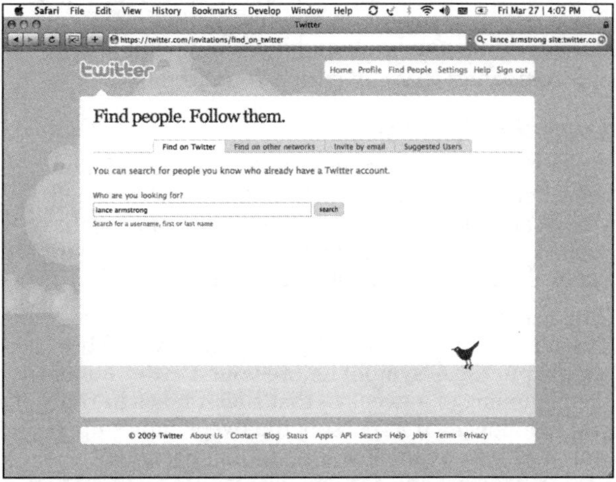

Figure 3-1: Search for Twitter users on the People Search page.

Another, lesser-known way to find people on Twitter is by simply using the Google search engine at `www.google.com`. Because Google indexes every public tweet, you can use it to find twitterers by interest or by name. To use Google to find twitterers that you might want to follow, either search on their full name and the word Twitter or do a slightly more specific search this way:

1. **Type your keywords or the username you're looking for in the text box.**
2. **Add** site:Twitter.com **at the end of your search query.**
3. **Click the Search button.**

   See what pops up! Figure 3-2 shows the results of a search for Lance Armstrong.

Figure 3-2: The Google results of a Twitter user search for Lance Armstrong.

TIP: You probably want to conduct people searches and keyword searches periodically to make sure that you continue to cultivate your Twitter experience's richness and value with new voices. Although Twitter is great for reconnecting with old friends and keeping up a conversation with existing business associates, it's also a fantastic way to reach out and find new people and companies to listen to.

REMEMBER: A great way to get started following people on Twitter is to import your contacts from your Web-based e-mail account (like Yahoo! Mail or Gmail). We cover this in detail in Part II.

Inviting people personally, through Twitter

Another option for inviting people to Twitter is to do it personally, directly to their individual e-mail addresses. You can find this tab (Invite By Email) on the Find People page (as shown in Figure 3-3), and it gives you a way to hand-pick people from your e-mail address book. You can also text Twitter at 40404 at anytime with the words **invite *yourfriend*@*yourfriend*.com** substituting your friend's e-mail address for *yourfriend*, of course.

REMEMBER: Keep in mind that Twitter doesn't offer you a chance to customize what the e-mail says. The person or company you invite gets a generic e-mail that mentions your Twitter handle and some basic information about how to sign up for an account. If you have people you want to invite to Twitter whom you think may not respond well to a generic e-mail, you can use the method described in the following section to invite them, instead.

Figure 3-3: The Twitter Invite By Email screen.

The main drawback to any of the invitation options in Twitter's Web interface is that none of them offer a custom message option. If you know people whom you want to invite, and you think they'd respond better to a private or more personalized note, just shoot them a normal e-mail that includes a link to the Twitter main page (`www.twitter.com`) and a note about why they might benefit from signing up and joining in. It's often more effective to e-mail them a link to an article that is going to help them understand what uses of Twitter they may find valuable. Twitter is definitely a minute-to-learn, lifetime-to-master type of system.

Opening up your stream

By default, Twitter shows you all the tweets sent by each of the users whom you follow. But sometimes, during the setup process, users accidentally limit their feeds to include only tweets that aren't replies — it's a neat feature, but not always desirable.

To configure your Twitter stream so that it shows you all the Twitter conversations that include @replies written by the people you're following follow these steps:

1. **Click Settings in the top-right navigation bar.**

   The Settings page opens.

2. **Click the Notices tab (see Figure 3-4).**

   You see an @Replies section, with a Show Me drop-down list.

3. **Select Show Me All @Replies from the Show Me drop-down list.**

   By setting this option, when your friends post public @replies to other Twitter users whom you aren't following, you still see those tweets.

Give yourself a little time to get used to the flood of information and figure out which @replies you want to see. You'll soon find that your friends not only have valuable things to say, but their friends do, too. At that point, you can start to join the conversation and broaden your circle of friends.

TIP: If you want your stream to be a little less crowded, you can opt to show No @Replies, which makes Twitter suppress any @replies from your stream. You won't see any @replies at all if you choose this option. A third, middle-of-the-road option is to select @Replies to the People I'm Following. What this means is that if you're following both John and Mary, and John sends an @Mary tweet to Mary, you'll see that tweet (even though it wasn't directed to you) — which allows you to join in the conversation because you can see what your friends are talking about. At the moment, these settings only filter tweets that start `@username`, not those that contain `@username` within the message.

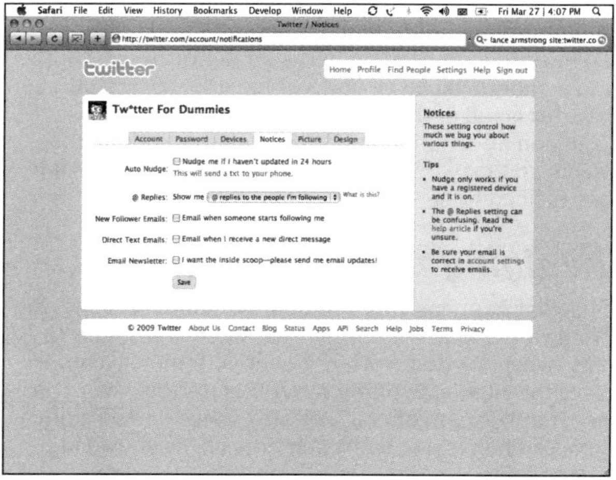

Figure 3-4: On the Notices screen, you can choose which, if any, @replies appear in your stream.

How to Follow People

Mechanically, following people on Twitter is dead simple. After you navigate to a person's Profile page, click the Follow button just below his avatar. You're done! Give it a shot:

1. **Browse to** `http://twitter.com/dummies`**.**
2. **Click the Follow button.**

   The button changes to the word *Following.* Cool!

Alternately, you can post this message from SMS or any Twitter interface by typing **Follow username** or **F username**.

Following people on Twitter is straightforward. On the most superficial level, you just have to pay attention. Twitter is full of thousands of great conversations going on all around you. If you open yourself up to them, you may find that hundreds of excellent people are thrilled to meet you.

Replying to Tweets

So, what happens when you receive an @reply and you want to respond — or if you just want to respond to any tweet, for that matter? Hover your mouse cursor over the right side of the tweet in question when you see it in your stream on Twitter's Home screen, and images of an arrow and a star appear (as shown in Figure 3-5).

Clicking the Star icon bookmarks that tweet as a favorite. But clicking the Arrow icon sets up the Twitter entry field so that you can reply to that individual tweet. When you send your response, it says In Reply

To below the tweet and includes a live link to the standalone page (also known as a *permalink*) for the tweet you responded to. Figure 3-6 shows a typical Twitter @reply.

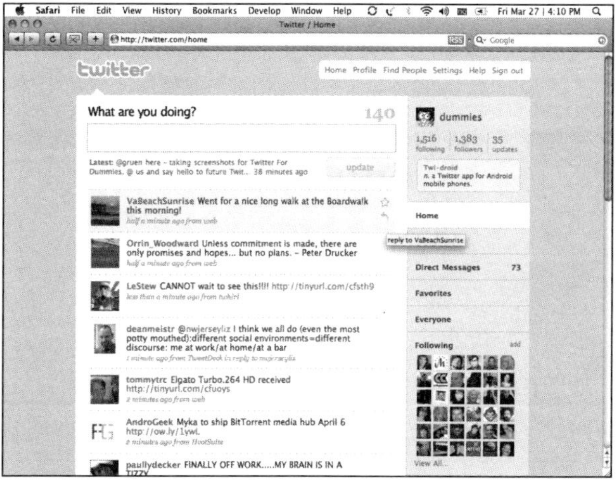

Figure 3-5: Don't miss the Reply arrow!

You may find these permalinks helpful because Twitter is not great at threading tweets together by conversation. If you're familiar with a set of @replies and the links associated with them, you can much more easily navigate the conversation later. When you know how to access the individual page for each tweet, you can also link to that tweet directly if you choose to respond to it in a longer format outside of Twitter, such as a blog post.

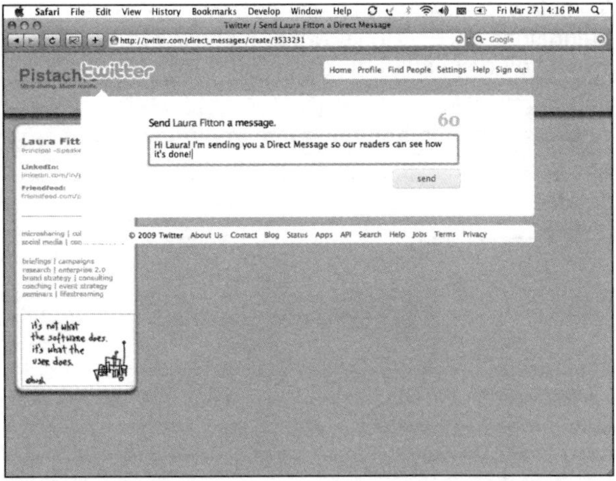

Figure 3-6: You can respond to tweets by using @replies.

You can reply to any tweet that you can see, and the procedure is the same, whether you're following the person or not. But, if your Twitter account is public, your @replies are public, too. If you want to use Twitter for private messages, the protocol is a little different, as we talk about in the next section "Direct Messaging."

Direct Messaging

Private messages on Twitter are called direct messages (DMs). Like any other kind of tweet, they're limited to 140 characters in length. You can't send a DM to someone unless that Twitter user is following you — likewise, only your own followers can send you DMs.

What do you do if you want to get in touch with someone privately on Twitter but that person isn't following you? New Twitter users are often tempted to send @replies to that person saying "tried to DM but you don't follow" or something of the sort. Some Twitter users don't mind receiving those kinds of tweets, but many others see them as rude or as blatant attempts to get new followers.

So, if you're trying to get in touch with someone who doesn't follow you, you have some options:

- **Check the user's Profile page.** See whether he has made available some other form of contact information — a Web site URL, an e-mail address, or a blog. You can often find this info in a user's short bio section.
- **Conduct a Web search.** Try searching for the user on your favorite search engine.
- **Tweet a polite question publicly to the user.** While the you-don't-follow-me approach is a little obnoxious, most twitterers will make a reasonable effort to respond if you respect their time and make it clear why they should answer you. Send a message to `@username` expressing why you're requesting their time and attention, and ask that they respond privately. Just try to differentiate between the ability to reach out to someone and the right to demand a response.

Direct-messaging shorthand

When you're truly connected, you start to find going to the Direct Messages page every time you want to send someone a message a bit tedious. Thankfully, the folks at Twitter have come up with a shortcut. To send a DM without going to the Direct Messages page follow these steps:

1. **Click in the What Are You Doing? window.**
2. **Type** d, **followed by a space, and then the username of the person to whom you want to send a direct message.**
3. **Type a space after his username and then write a message.**

   The update should have this form: d dummies Hey, there!
4. **Click the Send button to send the DM.**

Should I @ or DM?

When you try to decide whether to respond to somebody on Twitter by using a public @reply or a private DM, you should consider the following criteria:

- **Questionable content:** If your mother, grandmother, boss, or kid were looking over your shoulder at what you just started typing, would they be in any way embarrassed or disapproving? If the answer is yes, perhaps a direct message is in order.

- **Volume:** If you're a power user who posts to Twitter many times a day, every tweet goes into your followers' streams and contributes to the noise. You should be sensitive to this fact. If you tweet often, give your followers a break and save those one- or two-word responses, such as "@ pistachio LOL" or "@dummies How?" for a direct message.

Sensitive information: If you're supplying contact information, addresses, phone numbers, or other personal information that you don't want just anyone on the Internet to have access to, it's the right time for a direct message. Keep in mind that not everybody has the same standards regarding privacy and openness on the Web, so if you're sharing any information pertaining to anybody else's contact information or whereabouts, err on the side of caution and use a DM.

If you haven't protected your tweets, remember that whatever you write is indexed for all time. So, think twice!

Following Twitter Protocol

Many Twitter neophytes want to know what the rules are or whether Twitter has standard protocol and etiquette. Like many other social media sites, Twitter sprang from a close-knit group of early adopters who set the rhythm. Because Twitter was a favorite of Silicon Valley's new-media elite long before it broke into the mainstream, some insider jokes and conventions used can be confusing. Longtime users have certainly fallen into certain habits or sets of rules. But now that Twitter has become so popular and diverse, you can find plenty of wiggle room to do your own thing.

Like any other social-media company, Twitter has a Terms of Service (TOS) agreement that all members must adhere to or risk having their accounts suspended or deleted. You can access Twitter's terms at `http://twitter.com/terms`. You won't find anything particularly surprising in them: You must be at least 13 years old to create an account and use the service, you can't engage in abuse or harassment, you can't spam other members or participate in activities that break any laws, and so on. The terms are actually more liberal than most Web services' regulations; pornography and explicit language, for example, aren't banned.

Beyond the terms of service, Twitter etiquette is simple: Be genuine and nondeceptive and provide value. Other than that, just use Twitter how it suits you. This is primarily an unofficial protocol, but do keep in mind that Twitter keeps tabs on "deceptive" activity, too: Twitter can ban accounts that impersonate celebrities or companies if those accounts don't make it clear that they're unofficial or parodies. This policy is a contentious point in the Twitter community: Many members were upset when the `@cwalken` account, belonging to an aspiring comedian pretending to be actor Christopher Walken, was deleted from the system.

Beyond the simple regulations, you can't really use Twitter in a right or wrong way because no two people use it for exactly the same reasons. But some members certainly have their opinions:

- Some users complain when others tweet too often, whereas others complain that their contacts don't tweet enough. (This complaint is a little silly. Don't like the contents? Turn the dial. Unsubscribe.)
- Some users take issue with strings of @replies and wonder why those conversations weren't conducted in a private forum.

REMEMBER: You may encounter confusing, even conflicting, advice and back-seat tweeting from the handful of people on Twitter who aren't comfortable without rules. Don't take them too seriously; Twitter just isn't that rigid.

Be polite on Twitter, for the most part, but no more or less so than you're expected to be in the real world — just keep in mind that Twitter is a public forum. Twitter posts and feeds get exported outside of Twitter and onto Twitter-based Web sites, blogs, social-media sites such as Facebook, and aggregators such as FriendFeed. If you know you plan to, say, sync up your Twitter account with your Facebook account so that your tweets appear as your Facebook status message, keep in mind that you're branching out beyond the Twitter community and culture.

Although users love Twitter's largely rule-free nature, some generally accepted behaviors have evolved over time. You can ease your transition into the culture of Twitter by getting familiar with these behaviors before you first start out. Establish dedication and credibility early on, in part, by knowing your way around the following Twitter customs.

Language and abbreviations

Over time, any group of people that interacts regularly falls into its own "vernacular" way of talking. Twitter is no exception to that rule; in fact, it may be even more subject to it because of the 140-character limit. Twitter's lexicon has evolved over time to include unique words, phrases, and abbreviations that most regular users understand and recognize. But new users often find these references confusing.

Right off the bat, you see a lot of puns involving the word "Twitter," with the prefixes tw- or twi- added to the front: tweet, tweeple, tweetup, and so on. At first, it looks like baby talk — and indeed, it can get a bit over-the-top. Not all members are fans of corny terms such as tweeple. Others think the Twitter-specific language is fun, or an easy and obvious way to delineate something as Twitter-specific. Either way, whether you plan to use goofy Twitter-speak or not, it does help to know what this stuff means.

Many application and Web site names have adopted Twitter-speak words for products and services associated with Twitter or which tap into Twitter's application programming interface (API) to use Twitter data. For example, the word *twinfluence* was used casually to describe (no shock here) the kind of social influence that individual Twitter users had within the Twitter community. Eventually, the slang term was used to name twInfluence (`www.twinfluence.com`), an application that gets its data from Twitter and turns it into a report that estimates Twitter users' power and influence.

Plenty of eccentric people use Twitter, not to mention loads of subcultures and subcommunities. Just because you see an unfamiliar term doesn't mean it's part of the Twitter vernacular. For Twitter terms you should be familiar with, check out the glossary at the back of this book.

We purposely didn't include in this glossary some of the nonsense words that begin with the tw- prefix. Twitterers don't widely use them, many avid users actually find them rather annoying, and beginning to use them more often may be the first sign that you're a twitterholic!

Engaging others on Twitter

On Twitter, the name of the game is engagement. Whether you use Twitter for business or fun, you don't just want to sit back and watch the stream flow by — you want to genuinely interact with people. You have to know how to listen as much as know how to converse (this goes twice for businesses) — but it always boils down to engagement.

First and foremost, do not be shy about finding people who share your interests, even if you don't know them (yet). Use `http://search.twitter.com` to look for some of the most obscure keywords related to your work, hobbies, or passions. Then click through to the profiles of the people who wrote the tweets you find. You'll be amazed how good an idea you get of someone just by glancing at their last 20 tweets. Interested? Follow them. It's not like other social networks where you're really only expected to connect to folks you already know.

A great way to engage others on Twitter is to turn on the Show All @Replies option in your settings. If you have this option turned off, your Twitter feed doesn't display @replies directed to people who aren't in your network. If you turn this option on, you can see the whole conversation. The more tweets to other people you see, the more chances you have to "meet" new people, jump in, and engage.

While you sift through the Twitter conversation, don't be shy about clicking the usernames that you see (as in @replies) and writing to strangers offering your own opinion. It may take a few tries with a few different conversations before the chatting users include you in their conversation, but eventually they do.

But even if you don't @reply, your tweets still appear in search, and other Twitter users can spot them. If you have something interesting to say, people start to reply to your tweets. If you seek out and use relevant keywords and #hashtags, you will start to connect with others who share your interests. Your early days on Twitter will probably be pretty quiet when it comes to replies and conversation. All those twitterers are just getting to know you, after all. Don't worry; after a few of your tweets appear in the timeline and you add a few contacts to your network, people will begin to notice you.

Tweeting frequency

Twitter users tend to settle into a rhythm of tweeting frequency, often unconsciously, over time. Some Twitter users are considered noisy because they tweet so much, whereas others can come across as standoffish because they don't tweet frequently. So, how much is too much or too little? How often should you tweet?

A good rule when you're starting out is to post at least four or five tweets per day. You most likely find yourself tweeting much more often than that, but if you aren't yet fully comfortable with it, use that number to get started.

If you're using Twitter for your business, or you plan to link to your products or posts on your personal blog, find a balance between the number of tweets that promote yourself and the number of tweets that provide value. You might think of this balance as an actual ratio. For example, for every link of your own that you place on Twitter, send out at least five tweets that inform, engage, and converse. If conversation and engagement are your aim, you definitely want to keep a human voice in your Twitter stream at all times.

It's worth thinking about who you want to reach. People new to Twitter and only following a few get bowled over by frequent tweeters simply because it's all they see on their stream. A roaring chat with friends you already know is a fine use of Twitter, too, and would involve *many* more tweets a day than, say, a business user or someone just figuring out what they want to do with the platform.

Regardless of how you get people to follow you, make sure to keep your Twitter interactions genuine. What you post on Twitter and contribute to the conversation, along with your ability to listen, determines your authority more than any follower count ever could.

We can't stress the importance of listening enough. The more you listen and hear what people have to say, and then respond thoughtfully, the more you can find out about people and the more well-rounded your experience (and the experience of your followers) becomes. Listening is the golden ticket of Twitter — make sure to do it every day that you log in. And log in often.

Speak Spanish — the fun and easy way!
Spanish
FOR
DUMMIES
Dialogues from the book on audio C
A Reference for the Rest of Us!
Berlitz
Susana Wald
Your handy guide to everyday words and expressions
Spanish Phrases
FOR
DUMMIES
A Reference for the Rest of Us!

Su Doku
FOR
DUMMIES
Andrew Heron
Edmund James
A Reference for the Rest of Us!
Brain Games
FOR
DUMMIES

The #1 wine book — now updated!
Wine
FOR
DUMMIES
4th Edition
Ed McCarthy
Mary Ewing-Mulligan
A Reference for the Rest of Us!

Now updated and expanded!
Mix up hip and classy drink recipes from A-Z
Bartending
FOR
DUMMIES
3rd Edition
Ray Foley
A Reference for the Rest of Us!

Making Everything Easier!™
Guitar
ALL-IN-ONE
FOR
DUMMIES
8 BOOKS IN 1
• Guitar For Dummies, 2nd Edition
• Rock Guitar For Dummies
• Blues Guitar For Dummies
• Classical Guitar For Dummies
• Guitar Exercises For Dummies
• Songwriting For Dummies
• Music Composition For Dummies
• Music Theory For Dummies

Making Everything Easier!™
Superfoods
FOR
DUMMIES
Learn to:
• Purchase and prepare extremely healthy foods
• Improve your diet and live longer
• Increase your energy and control your weight
• Prevent disease and avoid costly trips to the doctor
Brent Agin, MD
Shereen Jegtvig, MS

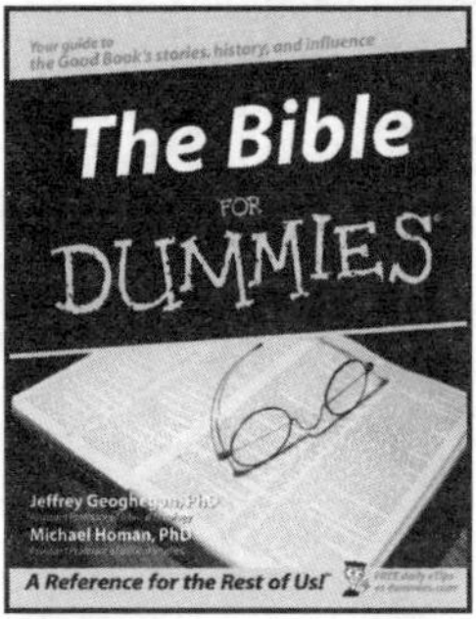
Your guide to the Good Book's stories, history, and influence
The Bible
FOR
DUMMIES
Michael Homan, PhD
A Reference for the Rest of Us!

"A gold mine of insight on the Catholic faith for people of all ages and beliefs."
Catholicism
FOR
DUMMIES
A Reference for the Rest of Us!

"A useful guidebook filled with clear instructions and helpful hints."
Meditation
FOR
DUMMIES
2nd Edition
Stephan Bodian
A Reference for the Rest of Us!

and living a more fulfilling life
Happiness
FOR
DUMMIES
W. Doyle Gentry, PhD
A Reference for the Rest of Us!

Making Everything Easier!
Personal Finance
FOR
DUMMIES
Learn to:
Eric Tyson, MBA

featuring coverage of the latest treatments
Diabetes
FOR
DUMMIES
3rd Edition
Alan L. Rubin, MD
A Reference for the Rest of Us!

Covers the iPhone, iPhone 3G, and iPhone 3G S!
3rd Edition
iPhone
FOR
DUMMIES
Learn to:
IN FULL COLOR!
Edward C. Baig
Bob "Dr. Mac" LeVitus

Making Everything Easier!
iPod & iTunes
FOR
DUMMIES
Learn to:
Tony Bove

Want more?

Visit **www.dummies.com/go/target** to get related articles, videos, or illustrated step-by-steps on your favorite Dummies title.

With more than 1,600 titles to choose from, we've got a Dummies Book for wherever you are in life! Look for Dummies titles wherever books are sold, call 877-762-2974, or visit *dummies.com.*